Music by CY COLEMAN
Lyrics by DOROTHY FIELDS

FRYER, CARR and HARRIS
present

GWEN VERDON
as

Sweet Charity

with
JOHN McMARTIN

JAMES LUISI   GLORIA MILLS
THELMA OLIVER   ARNOLD SOBOLOFF
and
HELEN GALLAGHER

Music by
CY COLEMAN

Lyrics by
DOROTHY FIELDS

Book by
BERT LEWIS

A New Musical Comedy
Based upon an original screenplay by
FEDERICO FELLINI

Scenery and Lighting by
ROBERT RANDOLPH

Costumes Designed by
IRENE SHARAFF

Orchestrations by
RALPH BURNS

Musical Direction & Vocal Arrangements by
FRED WERNER

Production Manager
ROBERT LINDEN

Staged and Choreographed by
BOB FOSSE

The cover is an authentic reproduction of the art used for
the original sheet music editions, first published in 1965

C • O • N • T • E • N • T • S

BIG SPENDER

Music by
CY COLEMAN

Lyrics by
DOROTHY FIELDS

CHARITY'S THEME

Music by
CY COLEMAN

Lyrics by
DOROTHY FIELDS

YOU SHOULD SEE YOURSELF

Music by
CY COLEMAN

Lyrics by
DOROTHY FIELDS

THERE'S GOTTA BE SOMETHING BETTER THAN THIS

Music by
CY COLEMAN

Lyrics by
DOROTHY FIELDS

14

WHERE AM I GOING?

Music by
CY COLEMAN

Lyrics by
DOROTHY FIELDS

I'M THE BRAVEST INDIVIDUAL

Music by
CY COLEMAN

Lyrics by
DOROTHY FIELDS

IF MY FRIENDS COULD SEE ME NOW!

Music by
CY COLEMAN

Lyrics by
DOROTHY FIELDS

TOO MANY TOMORROWS

Music by
CY COLEMAN

Lyrics by
DOROTHY FIELDS

THE RHYTHM OF LIFE

Music by
CY COLEMAN

Lyrics by
DOROTHY FIELDS

Moderately

Dad-dy start-ed out in San Fran-cis - co, toot-in' on a trum - pet loud and mean,

Sud-den - ly a voice said, "Go forth, Dad - dy, spread the pic-ture on a

wid - er screen." And the voice said, "Broth-er, there's a mil - lion pi - geons

BABY DREAM YOUR DREAM

Music by
CY COLEMAN

Lyrics by
DOROTHY FIELDS

SWEET CHARITY

Music by
CY COLEMAN

Lyrics by
DOROTHY FIELDS

I LOVE TO CRY AT WEDDINGS

Music by
CY COLEMAN

Lyrics by
DOROTHY FIELDS

March tempo

Lyrics:
I Love To Cry At Wed-dings, how I Love To Cry At Wed-dings, I walk in-to a chap-el and get hap-pi-ly hys-ter-i-cal, The ush-ers and at-tend-ants, the fam-i-ly de-pen-dents, I see them and I start to sniff, have you an ex-tra

I'M A BRASS BAND

Music by
CY COLEMAN

Lyrics by
DOROTHY FIELDS

48